THE SIMPLE GUIDE TO
CUSTOMS AND ETIQUETTE
IN
THAILAND

ABOUT THE AUTHORS

DEREK TONKIN was British Ambassador to Bangkok
(1986-89), and since retiring from the Diplomatic Service he
has become an independent Adviser on Vietnam, Cambodia,
Thailand and Laos.

VISNU KONGSIRI was educated at Charterhouse, RMA
Sandhurst and the University of California, Berkley. He is a
Director of Nibondh & Co Ltd and currently holds the rank of
Major General in the Royal Thai Armed Forces.

ILLUSTRATED BY
IRENE SANDERSON

THE SIMPLE GUIDE TO CUSTOMS AND ETIQUETTE IN

THAILAND

DEREK TONKIN & VISNU KONGSIRI

GLOBAL BOOKS LTD

Simple Guides • Series 1
CUSTOMS & ETIQUETTE

The Simple Guide to
CUSTOMS & ETIQUETTE IN THAILAND
by Derek Tonkin & Visnu Kongsiri

New edition 1996.
First published by
GLOBAL BOOKS LTD
PO Box 219, Folkestone, Kent, England CT20 3LZ

© Global Books Ltd 1996

ISBN 1-86034-045-8

British Library Cataloguing in Publication Data
A CIP catalogue entry for this book
is available from the British Library

Distributed in the USA & Canada by:
The Talman Co. Inc
131 Spring Street
New York, NY 10012
USA

Set in Futura 11 on 12 pt by Bookman, Slough
Printed & bound in Great Britain by
The Cromwell Press, Broughton Gifford, Wiltshire

Contents

Preface

The original 1990 edition of this book, entitled *Simple Etiquette in Thailand*, was written by Derek Tonkin, shortly after he returned to London, following a very successful period as British Ambassador in Bangkok from 1986-89. On publication, the book was very positively reviewed by the Thai press. Indeed, it reflected the author's great sensitivity and insight into the culture and language of the Thai people that was so widely appreciated during his term as Ambassador.

To be asked, therefore, by the new publishers, Global Books Ltd, to collaborate with the publication of a revised and expanded new edition was certainly something of a challenge; but also a great privilege. There was so little of the original that required any kind of change; it was more a question of what to add and update where I could in the hope of making the new edition fully reflective of Thai culture and traditions in the last decade of the twentieth century. I hope this has been achieved satisfactorily.

VISNU KONGSIRI
Bangkok, Summer 1995

THAILAND

1

The Land

'. . .never colonized by any Western country'

We used to know Thailand as 'Siam'. The country changed its name in 1939, reverted to Siam again for a brief period after the Second World War, but changed back permanently to Thailand in 1949.

The Thais themselves have called their country, in their own language, 'Thai-land' (*muang thai*, more formally *prathet thai*) for many

---

NOTE: 'Thailand' was devised just before the Second World War when Thai nationalism was particularly strong. Most scholars say that the term 'Siam' (possibly related to 'Shan' – Shan States in Burma) was a word originally used by Thailand's neighbours (Chinese, Burmese, Khmers) to describe Thailand. But some scholars have recently argued that Siam is, after all, a good Thai word.

centuries but Siam (*sayam*) has also been used as the formal name as well. Thailand, which means literally 'Land of the Free', is now the only correct international name, but Siam still appears in royal titles and in the names of some banks, companies and newspapers.

Thailand's neighbours include Burma to the West, Laos to the North, Cambodia to East and Malaysia to the South. Thailand, situated in the Tropic of Cancer, is about the size of France but has a population of about 60 million. There are four main regions: the North – mountainous, cool in the winter and home to numerous hill tribes; the North-East – an arid plateau bordered to the East by the River Mekong; the Centre – a fertile rice-growing region around Bangkok; and the South – rich in rubber, tin and lush vegetation and also home to many Thai Muslims.

Visitors to Thailand should be aware of a unique feature of the country's history: it was never colonized by any Western country. Over the centuries the Thais did battle with their neighbours, notably the Burmese and the Khmers (Cambodians). But from the thirteenth century onwards the Thais created a nation-state which has survived intact to this day. Thailand came under some pressure from Western trading nations in the seventeenth century. Two centuries later, during the hey-day of colonial expansionism, the British in Burma and Malaya and the French in Laos and Cambodia secured significant concessions in territory as well as trade. But the Thais, under the wise leadership of King Mongkut (Rama IV), 1851–1868, and King Chulalongkom (Rama V), 1868–1910, succeeded where almost all other South-East Asian nations failed, in preserving their independence.

The absence of a colonial past (though Thailand made sensible use of the services of numerous Western advisers, particularly from France, Britain and Germany) is important to an understanding of Thai mentality. Visitors are welcomed as equals. Racial and religious prejudice is virtually unknown. Buddhist tolerance goes hand in hand with intense national pride. Poised to become the next NIC (Newly Industrializing Country) in the Asia-Pacific region, Thailand has the natural and human resources both to enjoy the benefits of industrialization and to preserve its traditions and culture, blessed as it is with an economy balanced between light industry, agriculture and services.

Thailand's principal exports have been rice, rubber, manioc and canned goods, but in recent years manufactured products have overtaken traditional agricultural produce and include jewellery, integrated circuits, textiles and footwear. Thailand now exports bicycles to Britain and television sets to Germany.

Overseas visitors, especially those from the West, are known to the Thais as *farangs*. The word is most probably a corruption of 'Frank' and originally meant Caucasians from the ports of the Near East (and not 'French', as popularly believed, although the Thai word for

---

NOTE: In 1782 the crown was offered to one of King Tak Sin's generals, Chao Phraya Chakri who was crowned with the title of Rama I. The present monarch is HM King Bhumibol Adulyadej, the ninth monarch in the Chakri Dynasty, or Rama IX. (Many Thai Kings have used the name 'Rama', derived from the name of the hero of the Indian epic Ramayana. Rama was the archetype of the perfect ruler. The system of designating monarchs in the present Chakri dynasty as 'Rama' was created by King Vajiravudh, who became Raja VI. He renamed all previous monarchs Rama I–V).

France is *farang-saet*). It is also the Thai word for the guava fruit. As a guava/farang in Thailand, you can never escape your Western origins. Yet there are, inevitably, those earnest young Westerners on a longish stay in Thailand who desperately wish to assimilate and become indistinguishable from their Thai hosts. One has to wonder why. As a six-foot, blue-eyed Scandinavian, you are never going to merge with the local Thai population. The Thais much prefer you as you are!

Royal Palace

THAI ROYAL FAMILY

There are two institutions of which every visitor to Thailand should be aware. First, the Monarchy. The Thai Royal Family holds a very special place in the hearts of all Thai people, from the farmer working in his rice field to the head of an international business empire sitting behind his desk in a modern office building. You will find portraits of Their Majesties and other members of the Royal Family displayed prominently in every home and office. This is done not because of some personality cult as in a number of socialist countries, but because of the genuine love and respect that the Thai people have for the Royal Family, especially the present King who has devoted his entire life to improving the well-being of his subjects.

Any disrespect shown to Their Majesties, either by word or deed, will be met with a very strong reaction and could land you in real trouble. There was a story once about a foreign entertainment editor of a local English language newspaper who suggested keeping emergency money in your socks when going for a night out. But because Thai bank notes have an image of the King on them, this raised howls of protest and he had to issue an apology and retraction.

The King has a special anthem, called the Royal Anthem, which is played whenever he or his representative arrives or leaves a function or ceremony. It is also played when a toast is made to His Majesty's health. Although it is not the same as the National Anthem, it is given the same respect and you should stand up.

RESPECT FOR BUDDHIST RELIGION

The second institution of special importance in Thailand is the Buddhist religion for Buddhism is the major guiding influence of the Thai people. Behave modestly and sensibly in all matters concerning the Buddhist religion, especially when visiting temples. Always take your shoes off when entering the *Bot*, where the main Buddha image is housed and where the major ceremonies, such as ordination, take place. Remember to step over the door threshold (a raised horizontal piece of wood at the bottom of the entrance) as it is considered disrespectful to step on it. Do be careful, too, about taking photographs inside a temple. There may be restrictions.

Buddha images, no matter how large or small, how old or new, are considered sacred. This is because they pass through various ceremonies performed by senior monks. (Those that you see in shops around the Giant Swing near Wat Sutat are for sale and have not yet gone through these ceremonies.) Because they are sacred, you should not use them for decoration in homes or offices. There are also very strict laws governing the export of Buddha images and you should make sure that all documents are in order before attempting to do so.

2

The People

'Buddhism is the major guiding influence'

Thailand was settled over the centuries by waves of migration, including Khmers and Mons (from Burma) and various peoples from southern China. The Thais arrived from Yunnan in southern China in the tenth and eleventh centuries and by the thirteenth century had established the first Thai capital at Sukhothai, moving to Ayutthaya in the fourteenth century and to Bangkok in the eighteenth century.

Most Thais live in the countryside. A typical rural family will include grandparents, cousins, an uncle or aunt, even children of distant relatives. Living together under one roof encourages natural courtesy, tolerance and mutual respect, in the interests of social harmony. Urban households retain these traditional values, as far as practicable; invariably, there are relatives up-country and so most urban Thais retain, and enjoy, their links with the countryside.

From an early age, Thais are brought up to accept a code of social behaviour based on respect for superiors, parents, teachers and the elderly. Accordingly, the emphasis in relationships tends to be vertical, rather than horizontal; deference, avoidance of conflict, a desire to please are hallmarks of the Thai character. This has in the past encouraged patronage and somewhat limited the scope for advancement by merit. But as Thailand progresses economically and a sophisticated, urbanized population emerges, opportunities for personal advancement, particularly in the private sector, are increasing rapidly.

UNDERSTANDING BUDDHISM

The Buddhist religion has been a dominant influence, probably the most important factor, in the development of the Thai personality. Thai village life over the years has followed a cyclical pattern of farming which is reflected in a cycle of fixed Buddhist festivals throughout the year. Buddhism is a religion of simplicity and quiet contemplation. The Buddha, which means simply 'The Enlightened One,' was a prince who lived in Northern India 25 centuries ago (add 543 to the Western year to obtain the Buddhist year; AD1995, therefore, becomes BE2538 (Buddhist Era) in Thailand); he renounced material comforts in the search for enlightenment about the nature of human existence. In Thailand, Buddhism was enhanced by Brahminism, which brought colour, festivity and ritual to the religion and gave the Thai people a pleasantly practical interpretation of the Buddha's teachings.

On the whole, Thais are content to accept their lot without carping or resentment, though their approach to life is invariably positive, carefree and good-natured. There is perhaps a certain fatalism in their attitude, deriving from the Buddhist concept of 'karma,' which basically means 'action': the law under which your present life is determined by the cumulative merit of previous existences, and good deeds in this life will be reflected in your next life. Although materialist influences have in recent years had some impact, most Thais prefer a life of contentment and enjoyment to one of material acquisition.

Buddhism teaches that life is suffering, that earthly pleasures are only transient and that progress towards enlightenment and the attainment of eventual 'nirvana' (salvation) requires personal commitment. The acquisition of merit through good deeds helps to this end. Thais do not believe, however, that life should be taken all that seriously. As farmers, Thais know that rice cultivation is strenuous work and that life would not be all that much fun without some diversion and communal jollity. Ploughing, seeding, transplantation and harvesting would certainly be tedious without having a laugh. Work and play do indeed mix in Thailand, so much so that the word for work, *ngam*, is also the word for festival or fair; the common meaning is communality.

One of the first words you will learn in Thai is *sanuk* (pronounced sa-nook), which roughly translated means fun. No activity in Thailand is thought worth undertaking unless it is *sanuk*. When a friend tells you what he has been up to, you are almost expected to ask 'Sanuk mai?' or 'Was it fun?' The Thai life-style, whether in the town or the country, is geared to pleasurable activities. A night out with friends, a trip up-country, a visit to relatives, a walk to a temple at festival times will all be *sanuk*.

As activity frequently involves travel, another essential Thai expression is *bpai tiao* (pronounced by-tiaow, as in 'miaow'), which literally means 'to go on a trip'; we would say 'going out.' Thais love to travel, whether short or longish journeys, since travel involves socializing, seeing new faces, meeting up with old friends. An evening at the cinema, a walk across the fields, a visit to a fair, are typical examples of *bpai tiao* which can also include chatting up girls and a night out on the town. *Bpai tiao* is, by definition, almost certain to be *sanuk*.

Thais love to travel

SPIRIT WORLD

Another strong influence on the Thais is the unknown, the supernatural, the world of spirits. Thais have a strong sense of the inexplicable, an acute awareness of the mystery of nature. The clearest manifestation of this are the gaily-coloured spirit houses which grace most gardens and households and places of natural beauty or ominous interest like an outcrop of rocks near a temple or an accident-prone locality on a highway. The local guardian spirits are there by natural right; people are only incidental occupants of land and property and need to respect, and occasionally humour, the local spirits.

In daily life, many Thais take care not to upset the spirits who are thought to be born out of the souls of departed human beings. Some spirits are perceived more as ghosts (called *pee*), unpredictable and malevolent, the source of misfortune and chicanery, the cause of terror, illness and material loss. In north-east Thailand, spirit worship is especially active.

It is scarcely surprising that, in such an uncertain world, Thais take sensible precautions. As a basic rule of conduct, no human venture should be launched until the auspicious moment has arrived. No business undertaking is initiated, no marriage solemnized, no decision of substance taken until the precise time designated by astrological calculation has been reached. An invitation to the opening of a new branch office, for example, will indicate in the programme the precise minute at which the new venture will be most auspiciously launched.

Dreams, premonitions, intuitive knowledge are taken seriously. Good and bad omens are seen as portents of success and failure. Charms and amulets are worn by many Thais, the most popular type of amulet naturally being small images of the Buddha. Spells and incantations, mystic formulae and protective tattoos all help to subdue malevolent spirits, who can also be bribed to remain dormant or, temporarily, go away.

After all, since whatever you do and whatever precautions you may take may not achieve the desired result, it is better not to worry. *Mai bpen rai* or 'never mind' is heard on almost any occasion. Literally it means 'there isn't anything' and it is a bit like the French *ce n'est rien* and the German *macht nichts*. *Mai bpen rai*, however, is used so much more frequently than equivalent Western expressions that it suggests as much a state of mind, an extension of Buddhist philosophy and, to the Westerner, sounds even a little exasperating. Thais have learnt to relax in times of adversity and disappointment. They do not get over-excited, for example, if the train is late or if they are stuck in a traffic-jam on the way to the airport. No need to cry; better to laugh instead.

FAMILY STRUCTURE

The basic social structure in Thailand is the individual family; groups of families are associated in village communities. The family represents stability and security in an ever-changing, uncertain world. Loyalty to and respect for the family, to the village, to the monarchy and to the country are highly developed. This encourages a strong sense of national identity and pride.

Family ties are of the utmost importance in Thailand, and this is reflected in the specific title given to each relative. For instance, is Aunt Mary your father's younger or older sister? In Thailand you can tell immediately by the designation given to her. Some of the more important designations for relatives are as follows:

pee	–	Elder brother or sister
nong	–	Younger brother or sister
phoo	–	Paternal grandfather
yah	–	Paternal grandmother
dhah	–	Maternal grandfather
yaai	–	Maternal grandmother
loong	–	Elder brother of father or mother
bhah	–	Elder sister of father or mother
ah	–	Younger brother or sister of father
nah	–	Younger brother or sister of mother

However, these designations are often used colloquially for people who are completely unrelated. For instance, a young waiter or waitress may be called over to your table by using the designation *nong*.

3

Social Relations

'Thais are very sociable'

Thais are very sociable. You will find it fun (*sanuk*) getting to know them. But before doing so, you should try to learn something about their social codes.

GREETING

Thais greet each other very much as people do anywhere else in the world, with a cheery sign of recognition and a chat. The most usual greeting (and also a farewell), appropriate on almost all occasions, is *sawatdee* which literally means 'May you prosper'. It may be used at any time of the day or night. To be polite, men should add the word *krap* and women the word *ka*, so that for men it is

22

sawatdee krap and for women *sawatdee ka.*
Krap (in Bangkok often shortened to *k'ap*) and
ka, incidentally, are the nearest words you can
get in Thai to 'yes,' though they mean little
more than 'I hear you'. You can also say *sabai
dee,* which is closer to our 'How are you?', but
not so frequent as *sawatdee* except in the
north-east (and Laos).

Thais do not normally shake hands among
themselves, though they will shake Western hands because they know that is what
foreigners do. Custom, however, is slowly
changing and in recent years it has become
accepted practice for Thais to shake hands
among themselves on special occasions, for
example, when signing commercial contracts or
at prize-givings, particularly at sports meetings,
where both a *wai* and a handshake are in
order.

THE *WAI*

The traditional Thai greeting, and farewell, is
to raise both hands gracefully and unhur-
riedly, palm to palm, fingers together, and
close to the body, in what is known as the *wai*
(pronounced 'why'). Your fingertips should be
between your chin and the top of your nose,
but never higher than your eyes, unless the *wai*
is directed at a Buddha image or the King. It is
tempting, but mistaken, to regard this as the
equivalent of our handshake. In Thailand, to
wai means not only to greet and to say
farewell; more importantly, it means to pay
your respects. Therefore you will see Thais
giving a *wai* when they pass shrines or the
statue of a respected King. The higher you
raise your hands and the lower you bend your
head, the greater the respect you wish to

convey. A *wai* must always be acknowledged. This is normally done with another *wai*, but a nod or a smile is usually sufficient for children or those of lower status.

The '*wai*'

The *wai* is accordingly always initiated by the person whose status, for reasons of age or rank, is inferior to the person to whom respects are being paid. When you join your Thai International flight at London, Frankfurt, Sydney or Los Angeles, the exquisitely dressed Thai air hostess will always *wai* to you, and she will *wai* to you again when you leave the flight in Bangkok. She does not expect you to respond; a smile and a nod are all that is needed. When you arrive at your hotel, you are likely to be met with another *wai* as you enter. Again, do not try to respond; it is not expected and you will be at a loss about how to *wai* with your hands full of luggage.

A person who initiates a *wai* is likely to bend his head to a greater or lesser extent, depending on the status of the person receiving the *wai*. Note how members of the Thai Royal Family at religious ceremonies themselves *wai* to the Buddhist clergy and how the latter, because of their special status in society, do not themselves respond to a *wai* with any physical movement.

If you are staying in Thailand for any length of time, you will gradually learn how to make a *wai*. Watch a company Chairman responding to the *wai* made simultaneously by the members of his Board of Directors with his own collective *wai* while holding a bundle of papers in his right hand and his briefcase in his left hand, but somehow contriving to bring one hand close to the other without dropping anything. See how schoolgirls *wai* and at the same time bob in a curtsy to their teachers, how peasants raise their hands up to their foreheads when greeting a member of the Royal Family, how prominent personalities when seated hold their hands in a mid-way *wai* position of quiet contemplation and reverence while listening to a Buddhist recitation.

The golden rule for newcomers is to smile at all times, *wai* only when you are quite sure it is the right thing to do and watch closely how the Thais themselves play out this age-old ritual. The most serious mistake you can make is to wave your hands around in a *wai* to all and sundry, in the mistaken belief that because you have seen something similar in India, it is alright to do the same in Thailand. Thais will be too polite and too shy to correct you; but they will laugh at you, from embarrassment, and you will make a further mistake if you interpret their laughter as pleasure and delight.

THE THAI SMILE

Thailand is indeed known as the Land of Smiles. In the West, we smile because we have something to smile about. In Thailand, people smile naturally, out of sheer *joie de vivre* but also because they have been brought up from an early age to please. To some extent the Thai smile is designed to placate unknown and possibly hostile forces, particularly awkward, red-faced foreigners. So there is something defensive about the Thai smile, designed to put you at ease. Thais do smile, of course, and often laugh at jokes and comic situations, as we do in the West, but harmless personal misfortunes (like being splashed by a passing car or losing a coin down a drain) at which Westerners might chuckle in private, Thais will observe with an open smile on their faces. The intention is not to laugh at you, but to help you psychologically out of your misfortune by sharing your experience and suggesting subliminally that there could be worse calamities!

From this you will gather that Thais are inclined to smile when they are embarrassed. The car behind bumps into you. You get out to remonstrate. The Thai driver is smiling. You resist the temptation to punch him on the nose. Instead, you smile back. His smile is the Thai way of saying sorry. Your smile is your acceptance of his excuses. He will smile back again to say thank you. Three smiles with three different meanings. So tempers are kept on both sides.

Some visitors conclude from all this that Thais are adept at smiling their way out of almost any situation. I suppose, in some ways, this could be true. But after all, why not? Of course, if the driver behind you is driving a truck and demolishes half your car, he is likely to conclude that no amount of smiling will cool your anger; so the chances are that he will simply take to his heels, both to avoid the police and an unpleasant confrontation with you.

Finally, you will notice that nearly all Thai girls smile at you. This is not a 'come hither' appeal (in most cases). It is their way of looking prettier. After all, you would surely prefer smiles to scowls, laughter to grumpy frowns.

BODY MOVEMENTS

Thais are naturally graceful and seem in perfect control of their bodies. Westerners look clumsy, ungainly, uncontrolled and even uncultured. But then Thais are taught from an early age to control their physical movements whereas the emphasis in the West tends to be on free physical expression. Thai girls are taught the elements of traditional dancing, where the main elements are poise, decorum and restraint.

Perhaps the first thing you will notice about social interreaction in Thailand is what the Westerner calls 'high posture/low posture' relations. Traditionally, Thais show respect for elders and superiors by ensuring that they do not loom physically over those higher up the social ladder. So there is a lot of ducking of heads and apparent cringing, which is not cringing at all but solely a display of respect. It used to be standard practice to crawl in the presence of members of the Royal Family. These traditions remain in Thailand today and at all formal occasions Thais will ensure that their heads are below the level of the member of the Royal Family to whom they are speaking.

You make the greatest mistake if you interpret this formalized subservience as out of keeping with Thailand's blossoming democracy. Thais are much attached to their cultural rituals and suggestions from foreigners that such behaviour is 'undemocratic' will be dismissed out of hand. There was an incident once when the wife of a European military attache refused to curtsey to the Queen. She was ostracized by the rest of the Diplomatic Corps for showing such bad manners.

What you do with your head, hands and feet is, therefore, very important. The head (and hair) being the highest part of your body, are almost sacred. This is why a barber will give you a *wai* before cutting your hair. The feet, being the lowest, are profane. Pointing your feet at someone, particularly at his head, is regarded as insolent behaviour. It can be hard to avoid. Crossing your legs while sitting can lead to one foot unintentionally pointing straight at the head of someone sitting on the other side of the room. So when seated, try to remember not to cross your legs; worse still is to rest them on another chair or put them on top of your desk. You should also not step over any part of a person's body, including legs and feet. This may be difficult in a crowded airport waiting-room, but it will show your good manners.

As for your hands, try to keep them under control. Resist the temptation to pat youngsters on the back. Pointing with your fingers is not quite as bad as pointing with your feet, but control your natural (Western) inclination to do so. Men should never touch women in public. Of course, times are changing and where youngsters congregate, for instance in Siam Square near Chulalongkom

University in Bangkok, you may see daring youngsters of the opposite sex holding hands. You will, alas, also see foreigners (often overweight, balding, late middle-aged Westerners) holding hands with bar-girls; but that makes well brought-up Thai girls even more circumspect when going out with Western men.

Although the head is considered the most sacred part of the body, the heart (*jai*) is the centre of emotions and intellect. In English we say 'make or change our minds', but in Thai this would be 'make or change our hearts' (*dut sin* or *blien jai*). There are, in fact, so many phrases in Thai using the word '*jai*' that a book has been written trying to explain their meaning in English.

Things are never thrown in Thailand. They are always handed over, preferably with the right hand, and to show respect, with both hands, especially to monks and older people. It is sometimes amusing to see a Thai walk four or five yards just to hand you a pencil or eraser. This characteristic may be the reason why Thais are not very good at games such as cricket and baseball; because of lack of practice, they have difficulty in catching things. On formal occasions, a small gold-coloured round tray with pedestal (*pharn*) is used. If you are presented with something on a *pharn*, just take the item only.

KEEPING YOUR TEMPER

Buddhism is the Middle Path, the avoidance of extremes and violence, the attainment of harmony, inner and external. So Thai behaviour eschews displays of conflict and temper. Keeping a cool heart (*jai yen*) in all possible circumstances is not only ideal behaviour but the norm. Though angry and frustrated, Thais rarely give vent to their feelings. A hot head (*jai rawn* or hot heart) is a social lapse. Westerners are almost expected by Thais to lose their tempers at some point. Placating Thai smiles, alas, sometimes have the opposite effect. The maintenance of superficial harmony, however black your thoughts, may produce underlying psychological tensions which, when they do come to the surface, lead to violence. The Thai murder rate puts Thailand well up the international league. Avoiding conflict necessarily leads to some superficiality in contacts. Anger in any case might upset malevolent spirits.

Some Thais seem to get drunk easily, possibly because of their light body weight; but in such circumstances friends and even bystanders will try to placate the drunk or smile embarrassingly to excuse his behaviour. A drunken man is, after all, out of control. With a 'hot heart' he may (or malevolent spirits may induce him to) get up to all sorts of mischief, like tossing a hand-grenade at his rival in love, perhaps at a crowded fair-ground.

Like physical violence, verbal violence is equally unbecoming. Criticism is regarded as a form of verbal abuse. Irony and sarcasm are taboo. A dressing down, even in private, induces resentment. If behaviour is less than ideal, the vaguest of suggestions in due course about how matters might be improved is as far as most Thais would go. An employee dismissed for very good reason may harbour a grudge which could last for years and then suddenly lead to an explosion. A servant summarily dismissed for theft could harbour a long-standing resentment. As a visitor, you are unlikely to find yourself in such situations. But beware of shaking off tourist and night-club touts too physically; their friends may jump on you if you react too strongly to their propositions. At all times, a smile means you know the name of the game.

FACE

Much of what you have read in this chapter is about 'losing face'. Almost anywhere in the East, 'face' is important. There is probably no need to go into further detail here, except to say that Thais will go to great pains to ensure that, so far as possible, you do not lose face. It is almost as though saving the face of others is more important than the risk of losing your own.

'Things are never thrown in Thailand'

4

Festivals & Weddings

Festival of Loy Krathong

Thailand has many festivals throughout the year, but the two most popular are Songkhran and Loy Krathong, which are celebrated throughout the country.

SONGKHRAN

Traditionally, this festival celebrates the Thai New Year. It falls on 13 April and lasts for three days. Household Buddha images are cleaned and family members get together to pay their respects to family elders. This is done by presenting them with some small gifts, usually towels or a piece of cloth, and pouring scented water over their hands. Consequently, there is a mass exodus from Bangkok by people returning to their homes in the provinces, and all road, rail and air transportation is fully booked. If you have to go to the airport on 13 April, make sure you allow plenty of time. The highway to the airport is also the main highway to the north and northeast and mammoth traffic jams are inevitable, and the forty-minute trip may take three or four hours.

Since Songkhran occurs in the hottest month of the year, it has become a tradition to throw water over complete strangers. Pretty Thai girls or Westerners dressed in T-shirts are usually the main targets and everything is done in the spirit of fun or *sanuk*. Whereas formerly water was thrown from small bowls, high-powered water pistols and buckets are now used. Be prepared for a drenching if you venture out into the streets during this time, especially in the Banglampoo area.

Incidentally, the Western New Year, 1 January, is also celebrated in Thailand in much the same way as in other countries. It has become a tradition to send New Year cards and to present respected elders (family or business) with baskets of fruit or hampers of groceries. These can be obtained at all department stores prior to the New Year and vary in price depending on the contents (which may include XO Brandy and other luxury imported goods). Banks and businesses give away promotional material, such as calendars and diaries, to their clients. Servants are also given a monetary bonus.

LOY KRATHONG

In former days, rivers and canals played a highly significant role in the daily life of the Thai people. They were the source of water for domestic and agricultural use and provided fish for the table, as well as providing an essential method of transportation and a convenient way of waste disposal. *Loy Krathong* is the Thai people's way of thanking and asking forgiveness from *Mae Kongkha*, the Mother of Waters.

This festival takes place on a full moon night in October or November, when the water in the rivers is at its highest level. 'Loy' means to float, and 'krathong' is a small cup usually made of banana leaves. An incense stick, a candle, a coin and flowers are placed in the *krathong* which is then floated down the river. The sight of hundreds of *krathongs*, with their flickering candles, floating down the river under a full moon is truly magical.

'Spirit shrine'

WEDDINGS

There is no religious ceremony for weddings in Thailand comparable to the church wedding in the West. Although food may be offered to monks in the morning, the Thai wedding is almost a totally secular affair, and can be divided into three distinct activities.

The couple are legally married when they register their marriage at the local district office; if the families are important enough, then the Registration Officer may be invited to the house to register the marriage. The second activity is blessing the bridal couple, and this is what is usually demonstrated at Thai cultural shows performed for tourists.

The bride and groom, dressed in traditional Thai costumes, kneel side by side in a semi-erect position, with their heads slightly bowed and their hands held in front of them in a *wai* position. Their heads are joined together by a thick white cotton thread, called a '*mongkol*', symbolizing their union. Guests then take turns in pouring scented water over the hands of the bride and groom. This is usually done with a decorated conch shell, but sometimes a small silver bowl is used.

These two activities, the registration and pouring of scented water, can take place at any time of the day, depending on the auspicious time worked out by astrologers, and are usually attended by close friends and relatives. However, the third activity, the reception, is usually held in the evening and attended by all friends and acquaintances of the families concerned.

It is to the reception that you will probably be invited. This usually takes place at about 6 pm in the ballroom of a major hotel. In front of the reception hall you will find a long table where you present your gift, which could be money put into the envelope in which you were sent your invitation (this is an easy way of identifying yourself), or any other traditional wedding gift, such as a photo album. Then you sign the reception book and receive a memento of the wedding. The bride and groom, with their parents, stand in line ready to greet you as you enter the reception room.

Weddings are a great place to meet friends and business contacts, and it is quite proper to wander around. When all the guests have arrived, representatives of the bride and groom will make speeches and wish them a long life of wedded bliss; then the bride and groom thank the guests for coming, and this is usually the sign that you can leave. At the door you will again find the bride and groom and their parents ready to bid you farewell.

5

Food & Eating Out

'. . .the sheer variety which appeals to foreigners'

Thais love eating; indeed, they seem to spend most of their waking hours nibbling at anything they fancy. With 60 million potential customers, restaurants of all shapes and sizes spring up, if needs be, overnight. Itinerant vendors, sometimes pushing a ramshackle cart or even carrying a food kitchen balanced on a bamboo pole, are everywhere.

If a new building-site opens up, within 24 hours a lean-to shack restaurant will appear, as if by magic, selling noodles, curry and banana fritters. If the food is good, you will see quite respectable people sitting down for their midday meal at very modest pavement kitchens, just a few wooden stools and a couple of rickety, plastic-covered tables.

Thai food has developed remarkably over the last 20 years. It was always there, of course, but it is the sheer variety which appeals to foreigners. So many rice dishes, fish and seafood in so many variations, soups which are a meal in themselves. The variety of Thai food no doubt stems from the fact that Thailand has been a crossroads of the East, with the cuisines of India, China and Malay-Indonesia making their own particular contributions.

Eating in Thailand can be divided into three major categories: snacks, single-dish meals and multi-dish meals. These in turn can be sub-divided in noodles, rice dishes, Thai, Chinese, Indian, etc.

TYPES OF FOOD

Snacks

If someone were to ask me what is the favourite Thai pastime, I would have no hesitation in replying 'eating', and this is manifested in the hundreds of snacks, mostly sold by street vendors, that are available everywhere and range from chicken on skewers to fresh guava, pineapple, water-melon, grilled and fried bananas, etc. Try them, and you will be surprised at the difference between what you can buy in the West and the 'real thing'.

Single-Dish Meals

These are usually eaten for lunch by the local people and are equivalent to the 'fast foods' of the West. There are two main categories – rice dishes and noodles. Rice (kao) dishes consist of a plate of rice with a topping, such as chicken with basil, various curries, red or crispy pork and duck. Noodles (*guey-tiel*) come dry (*haeng*) or in broth (*nam*). There are four main types: large (*sen yai*), small (*sen lek*), tiny (*sen mee*) and egg (*sen ba-mee*). Won ton is known as *giew* in Thailand.

There are so many combinations of rice and noodle dishes that it would be impossible to list them all. One way to try them is at 'Food Centres' located in all major shopping centres. Here there is a common dining area with 20 or 30 booths selling different single-dish meals. The plates and cutlery are supplied by the shopping centre and you have to buy coupons (usually about 100 bahts worth and are valid only on the day of purchase) at strategically located counters. You can then wander round and select whatever takes your fancy. Unused coupons can be refunded for cash, but only on the same day. A good example of this type of Food Centre is located on the top floor of the Mah Boon Krong Shopping Centre.

Multi-Dish Meals

This is the way that Thais eat at home or in restaurants. Each person is given a plate of rice and there are three or four communal dishes of vegetable, pork, beef and fish which are placed at the centre of the table. Each person takes what he wants, usually from one dish at a time, and eats it with his rice. This is very practical as you take only what appeals to you, and may have given rise to the famous 'Eastern hospitality', because if an unexpected visitor arrives, all you have to do is add an extra plate of rice and he can join the meal. In the West, if you have four pork chops for four people and someone arrives unexpectedly, what do you do?

In Chinese restaurants, guests usually sit at a round table with a revolving top. Food is served in courses and each course is eaten in turn. At more formal dinners, a waiter will serve each guest, but normally, guests serve themselves. Sometimes you may find your neighbour serving you, but this is quite normal and you should return the compliment. There are usually about eight or nine courses, and in Thailand, you know you have come to the last course when fried rice is served.

An increasingly popular type of meal is the Buffet Lunch or Dinner. These are usually provided by hotels and the advantage is that a large variety of dishes are available – Thai, Japanese and Western. For instance, the lunch buffet at the Siam City Hotel has a number of Thai dishes, a roast, salads, cold cuts, sashimi, sushi, fresh oysters, smoked salmon, etc., all for about 350 Baht ++ (the ++ after a price means plus service charge and plus government tax).

At restaurants serving Thai food, a fork and spoon are the only eating utensils. Chopsticks are generally used for noodles and at Chinese restaurants. Knives are rarely used when eating non-Western food. The fork and spoon you use will, incidentally, last you throughout the meal, whether the dishes change from spicy ('hot') to sweet and sour, salty or pungent. Dishes may be served piping hot, but are eaten even when cold. Make sure you know which sauce goes with which dish as sauces (or 'nam jim') can make all the difference to a meal.

Thais appreciate good food, but they do not belch or lick their fingers in public. You should begin eating as soon as the food is put in front of you. Conversation is considered proper during meals.

Some Thai food can be very spicy; peppers can be bad enough, but some chillies will take the roof off your mouth and bring tears to your eyes. If this happens to you, take some water and counteract the spice with plain rice or some sweet dish, even a spoonful of sugar. If you are drinking beer with your meal do not attempt to 'cool down' by drinking more of it: instead you should not touch a drop for at least five minutes!

WHO PAYS?

If a Thai invites you to a restaurant, he will naturally expect to pay. You will notice that he does not leave a tip, except perhaps a few baht for the waitress. This is because a service charge is invariably included or assumed to be included and, in any case, tipping is not a widespread custom. If you go on a business trip to Thailand, it could be that you should pay if you are the most senior person present.

Guessing the status of other people is one of the more sensitive social preoccupations of Thais and so much depends on your assessment of the age, family connections and wealth of others present, and their assessment of you. Potentially, much 'face' is at stake, particularly if you or your colleagues get it wrong. As a person of status, you are expected to do the honours and your failure to do so, or to offer only to split the bill, will not only make you lose status in the eyes of your Thai hosts, but may cause offence as well. If you wish to retain respect, be prepared to pay as required.

From all this, you may perhaps have concluded that status and respect may be bought in Thailand. Sadly, this is true in many cases, and the desire to acquire money, and thereby status, has undermined many traditional values. Hence the rise in sex-related activities, such as prostitution, massage parlours and bars, where money can be obtained quickly and easily. In a society where prostitution is endemic, many young women aspire to money because money brings power and power brings status. Money is the means to social redemption; the loss of face in prostitution may be more than compensated for by the acquisition of the means to improve one's status eventually.

VISITING THAI HOMES

Despite the emphasis on eating out, you may occasionally be invited to a Thai home. Even in modern apartments, the rule is to take off your shoes. It is mainly a token of respect and not so much a desire, as Westerners tend to assume, not to bring dirt into the household; it is also much cooler without shoes on. You will probably sit on chairs, but you might also be invited to sit on the floor. Try not to sit cross-legged; sit on your heels if you wish; better still, tuck your legs under you on one side, supporting yourself if you must with one hand. Try not to sit against a wall with your feet pointing out.

GIFTS

Take a small present for your host, who may give you one in return. Flowers are always welcome, or a box of local confectionary/cookies, or some attractive small ornament: it need not be large and expensive. It is the thought that counts. Thais themselves love presents; they are often beautifully wrapped with pretty ribbon. It used to be thought bad form to open presents straight away, but this taboo is less strict nowadays and, if invited, you may take a look. On balance, though, it is better to put the present aside until later, unless you are quite sure it would not cause offence by opening it up there and then.

If you are staying overnight, spare a thought for the house spirits. There is in particular the Lord of the Place (Phra Phum) who has his shrine in the compound and there are possibly other spirits of the locality, normally at least another eight. I once slept*, unawares, in a room haunted by a malevolent spirit, but as I was a foreigner, I had nothing to worry about.

'. . .spare a thought for the house spirits'

---

* Co-author Derek Tonkin

6

Business & Entertainment

'Eastern mysteries'

BUSINESS CULTURE

The rules about social behaviour and entertaining apply very much to business
relations as well. Because Bangkok is such a
sprawling metropolis and the traffic at times so
exasperating that it can take you well over an
hour to get across town, you will probably find
that you can, with luck, make only two business
calls in the morning and only one in the
afternoon. This tends not to leave all that
much time for entertaining your business
contacts, even if you and they would like to
get together.

Business lunches are very acceptable and the better-class restaurants provide a crisp, but relaxed service. As many Bangkok businessmen leave home at 6.00 or 6.30 in the morning, they are usually ready for lunch at 12.00. Many people, especially government officials, leave for lunch at 11.30. Thais on the whole prefer Thai or Chinese food, but will gladly eat Western food if the opportunity occurs. (For some reason, lamb and mutton have a very strong smell for Thais, and they usually cannot eat it unless it is smothered in spices.) As mentioned earlier, nearly all hotels have buffet lunches and these are popular as they cater for all tastes. Nouvelle cuisine is still very much in vogue at the top-class restaurants like the Normandie Grill in the Oriental Hotel and Le Cristal at the Regent. Low calorie, salad-oriented business lunches for the health-conscious businessman are catching on only slowly.

Inviting your business contacts out to an evening meal needs careful judgement. On the whole, Thais like to get away from the office by 4.30 or 5.00 at the latest and are frankly not all that interested in hanging around in town until dinner time, which can be as early as 6.30. If your associates are sufficiently senior and Westernized, they will understand the importance of relaxed entertainment when those controversial clauses in the deal under negotiation can perhaps be finally agreed. However, although they may be too polite to say so, a formal dinner is likely to be, for most except Board-level representatives, something of an ordeal. If you can contrive more informal entertainment in very casual attire (buffet dinner on a river launch, a private room in a popular restaurant), this is likely to find far greater favour with your Thai guests.

Everyone in Thailand has a business card, even the management trainees. There is no need to bring a great quantity with you as you can have them printed very easily in Thailand. Simple cards with no company logo can be printed in half an hour at any major shopping centre. More complicated cards will need a professional printer but the service is very fast, efficient and inexpensive. Insist on examining the proofs and do so very carefully as mistakes can be time-consuming and hard to rectify.

Some years ago it used to be fashionable to have your cards printed in Thailand in English on one side and in Thai on the other, but this practice is waning as knowledge of English increases and, frankly, is no longer either necessary or desirable. Most Thais (and even some Westerners!) acknowledge that spelling in any language is only a rough guide to pronunciation, so that your English-language visiting card is adequate in itself. But do try and include as much detail as possible, including your telephone, telex, fax and even home number. It helps to build up your status and personality.

EASTERN MYSTERIES

Finally, a word of advice about those special payments which some say are essential to doing business out East. Find yourself a reliable local agent and listen to his advice. Should he feel that for any reason it might be prudent to offer a commission, technical fee, research charge, agency split or any other euphemistic payment, let him attend to this in his own way. Above all, do not let yourself get involved in passing money in brown paper envelopes under the table to individuals who have somehow convinced you that the secret of success lies in their personal remuneration on the side. You will invariably pass the wrong sort of money, at the wrong time, to the wrong people.

Instead, take the perfectly respectable view that, as a Westerner, you cannot possibly begin to understand these mysteries. All local firms have local fixers. Never forget that, for public sector contracts, there is a formidable Counter Corruption Commission which can (and does) descend on unwary public servants and take them and their books away for minute investigation. You should also know that some of the most successful Western firms in Bangkok have never ever resorted to illegal payments, precisely because there are so many legal ways in which these delicate matters can be satisfactorily resolved, to everyone's mutual satisfaction.

A NIGHT OUT ON THE TOWN

Thais can be very hospitable, even lavish with their entertainment; it enhances their status and they regard money spent on having fun (*sanuk*) as money well spent. They will not expect you to reciprocate in Thailand, nor to 'stand the next round'.

Bangkok's night life is world famous. Provided you watch your spending, a night out on the town can be relatively inexpensive. There are a thousand-and-one distractions for males. For couples, the flashy discos and more intimate videotheques, the jazz and dixie-land night spots, even the go-go bars can be a lot of fun. Women are welcomed, and safe, almost anywhere, but are unlikely to want to stay for the duration. As a single woman, it is best to go in company; two women can enjoy the scene, but not much else.

Most males make their way to Patpong, three street blocks in an area between Silom and Suriwongse Roads. Patpong 1 and 2 cater principally for Western and English-speaking tourists, Patpong 3 for Japanese. There are a range of ground-floor bars, with gyrating go-go girls, the music not quite as ear-splitting as in the discos. The bar-girls will chat you up, but not pester you. Their English is limited. You can stay for about half an hour on one beer (Baht 60) and a coke (Baht 50) or two for the girl who sits with you. [Note: The current rate is Baht 25 = $1]. You can then move on to another ground-floor bar, or venture upstairs to one of the first-floor establishments which have even more scantily-dressed girls and will offer floor shows as well. Prices are double, if not treble, the ground-floor establishments and what you see, particularly during the floor shows, may make your eyes pop, so I suggest that you do not go upstairs if you are easily shocked.

Apart from Patpong, there are similar complexes at Soi ('lane') Cowboy and at the Nana Entertainment complex. You might also try a massage, either traditional style (perfectly respectable) or at one of the tourist massage parlours (where anything goes). The larger massage parlours along Petchaburi Road nowadays mostly cater for locals and some masseuses are reluctant to take on Westerners because of growing concern about AIDS.

The bar-girls and masseuses who service the tourist industry have become something of a legend. By and large, they are not the kind of toughened hustlers who operate in West European countries. Most of them come to

Bangkok hoping to make about Baht 100,000 over five years, enough for them to return home up-country and open a dress-making shop or beauty salon, and hopefully to settle down and marry (a second time: their first marriage is generally disastrous, which may be why they came to Bangkok in the first place). They will laugh and cry with you, but some of them are not as sophisticated as they seem and are learning about AIDS the hard way.

Dotted around Bangkok are what are described as 'Member Clubs'. These are for local businessmen, not for foreign tourists. As a casual visitor, you will pay through the nose, so do not venture inside unless you are taken by a Thai friend at his expense.

One final word of advice: if ever you find yourself being hustled by a bar owner, do not react violently, but as soon as you get outside, ask for help from the ever-watchful Tourist Police and, without to much trouble, you will get your money back.

'. . .even lavish with their entertainment'

7

Travelling in Thailand

Tuk-tuk

A s a visitor to Thailand, you may wish to do some travelling on your own. The main domestic airline, Thai Airways, now amalgamated with Thai International, has frequent services to all major destinations in Thailand (Boeing 737s and Airbus). In Bangkok, the domestic terminal is next to the international terminal and a free shuttle service is provided. Another domestic airline, Bangkok Airways, flies to a number of destinations, of which the most popular is Koh Samui, the resort island in the Gulf of Thailand. There is also a good railway network and buses and coaches of all description. Be careful when travelling during major holidays, such as Songkhran and the New Year, as all means of transportation are fully booked.

TAXIS AND TUK-TUKS

Nearly all taxis in Bangkok now have meters, although some drivers are reluctant to use them. Initial fare is 35 Baht. No tip is expected, but the passenger has to pay any expressway fees. Most major hotels have a limousine service which can be hired for the day or for a specific destination; naturally, they are much more expensive than taxis.

'Tuk-tuks', or motorized three-wheel scooters, are popular with back-packers but they do not provide much protection from the elements or the pollution of Bangkok. Fares must be agreed upon before starting the journey, so do not get into the tuk-tuk before this is done. Many tuk-tuk drivers are young men from the Northeast and cannot resist the lure of an open road, so some journeys can be hair-raising.

As most taxi and tuk-tuk drivers know very little English, the major problem is making your destination known. The easiest way to overcome this problem is to ask a Thai to write down the destination for you. Never hail a taxi or tuk-tuk with your foot.

Motorcycle taxis are a relatively new method of transportation which has evolved as a result of the traffic situation in Bangkok. Formerly, they were used to take passengers from the main road to their destinations in the small lanes that are not serviced by buses. However, when the traffic is at a standstill, which is quite often, they may be the only means available of reaching your destination in time. Helmets are compulsory on the main roads, but motorcycle taxis always have a spare one for their passengers. As sitting on the back of a motorcycle weaving through dense traffic can be heart-stopping, this method of transportation should only be used in dire emergencies.

BUSES AND BOATS

There are four types of buses in Bangkok: executive, air-conditioned, ordinary and green. Executive buses are limited to about 20 seats (no standing) and have air conditioning, TV, newspapers and telephones. There is a flat rate of 25 Baht per trip irrespective of distance. Unfortunately, there are not too many routes but more are being planned. Air-conditioned buses have more routes but tend to be more crowded. Fares start at 6 Baht and depend on the length of the journey. Ordinary buses are the principal means of transportation in Bangkok and consequently can become very crowded, especially during the morning and evening rush-hours. Fares are 3.5 Baht per trip. Green buses are privately owned and have a concession to supplement ordinary buses. Fares are 2.50 Baht per trip. Maps with bus routes can be purchased at bookstores.

Another way of getting around is by boat and there are frequent services along the Chao Phaya river. Most landings supply you with details of the service. Passenger ferries also cross the river at strategic points and cost one Baht per trip.

Buses also connect Bangkok with nearly every part of the country. Some are very comfortable but it can become very crowded when there are holidays. There are three terminals which serve different regions: Northern Bus Terminal (Mor Chit) for the North and Northeast; Eastern Bus Terminal (Ekkamai) for the East and the Southern Bus Terminal (Pin Klao) for the South.

When travelling on buses, whether in the city or up-country, it is customary to give due respect to monks. Try to give them space; women must never come into physical contact with them.

TRAINS

Trains are another popular way of travelling up-country. However, trains are slower than buses and routes are limited. Overnight sleepers to popular destinations such as Chiang Mai and Haad Yai are well patronized. The same rule concerning monks applies to trains as well as buses.

CARS

Cars may be hired. As in Britain (and Malaysia, Singapore, Indonesia, Hong Kong and Japan), cars drive on the left. The speed limit in towns is 60 kms per hour and 100 kms per hour in the country. After overtaking, you are expected to move back into the left-hand lane; there is generally no 'slow' lane as in Europe, unless it is specifically designated. Most road signs are in Thai, warning signs included. You may feel it better to hire a driver as well, which will only add another 25–30 per cent on the cost of the hire. If you do want to drive yourself, a valid international driving licence is required.

Be warned that up-country heavy trucks will not necessarily get out of your way on narrow roads and bus drivers sometimes drive too fast trying to meet schedules in very difficult conditions. There have been some appalling accidents. If you are involved in a minor accident, as a foreigner you are assumed to be richer and so are expected to pay (your higher status, hence your privilege). In more serious accidents, the other driver is likely to have the advantage of speaking fluent Thai, but he might flee the scene if he has no licence or is blatantly in the wrong.

Hire cars only from hotels and reliable agencies. Even then, check on insurance. Beware of hiring motor-cycles at holiday resorts. They may not be insurable and could be technically defective. Sadly, many young foreigners do themselves serious injury on these contraptions.

Bangkok traffic is becoming more and more aggressive as more cars and more motorcycles compete for limited road space. Traffic jams in Bangkok are notorious and you can be stuck in one place for two or three hours. Although both short- and long-term remedial action, such bus-lanes, one-way roads, expressways, mass transit systems. etc., are being undertaken it will be some time before the situation improves.

Be warned also that pedestrian crossings (zebra crossings) are not inviolate as in some Western countries. Cars may not stop, so be extra careful when crossing roads. It is always advisable to use overpasses whenever possible. Beware also of motorcycles and buses coming from an unexpected direction in bus lanes.

CLOTHING

Westerners visiting Thailand will find the climate hot and Bangkok can at times be particularly oppressive and debilitating, so clothing should be light, loose and airy. Thailand has a booming ready-to-wear market, so a lot of good quality inexpensive clothing can be purchased locally. Thais are modest in clothing and most prefer to cover up against the sun when outside. Foreigners, on the other hand, tend to undress as far as they dare even in town (and at beaches more than they should). Natural fibres, such as cotton, are much to be preferred to synthetics. Most men wear short-sleeved shirts when at leisure, but long sleeves are sometimes worn in better-class restaurants, where the air-conditioning can be fierce. You will rarely see Thai women with bare shoulders, and too flimsy dresses in air-conditioned establishments can ruin an evening.

It is not too difficult to spot the less culturally-conscious visitor to Thailand. He could well be wearing shorts which reveal hairy legs while his chest is covered by a string singlet. His huge physical frame (occasionally with a beer belly) makes him appear slightly grotesque to Thais. She might be wearing a mini-skirt or shorts and something skimpy above. This lack of modesty is regarded by Thais as thoroughly bad taste. But tourism is an important money-spinner (some five million tourists now bring in around US$2 billion annually), so allowances are made; in any case, as a foreigner, you are likely to find yourself paying rather more in entrance fees to various establishments than the locals, an issue which gives rise to perpetual controversy in the local English-language press.

Westerners who live in Thailand for any length of time soon adapt to the sartorial customs of the country; light-weight trousers (pants) for men, sports shirts and fairly sturdy sandals. At the beaches, topless bathing is just possible in some areas (parts of Phuket and offshore islands like Ko Amui and Ko Samet), but most Thais regard it as silly; who wants to get sun-burnt and invite skin cancer? Thai girls go to great lengths to keep the sun off their skin; the paler their skin, the greater their imagined beauty.

VISITING TEMPLES

As noted earlier, one of the most attractive features of Thai culture are the Buddhist temples to be found all over the country, even in smaller villages. In Bangkok and other towns, the temples (*wat*) can be very elaborate, ornate constructions. The most important building in a *wat* is the *bot*; this is where the main Buddha image is housed and where important ceremonies, such as ordinations, are performed. Monks usually practise meditation, hold meetings and preach sermons in *viharn*. The *kuti*, or monks' living quarters, are off-limits to women. Other buildings may house Buddha images donated to the *wat* over the years. These images do not represent the Buddha as a deity, but are meant to help the individual through contemplation of the image's serenity, in his progress towards enlightenment. Nevertheless, all Buddha images, no matter the size, should be treated with the utmost respect.

While Thais are tolerant for the most part when foreigners 'put their foot in it,' they are likely to be seriously upset by unseemly tourist behaviour in temples; wearing a singlet and shorts when visiting a *wat* would be thought very bad taste and you might be asked to leave. Pay attention to any restrictions on photographing within the *bot*.

Visitors to temples should remove their shoes before entering the building containing the principal Buddha image. the intention is to show respect to the Buddha, no more, no less; it has nothing to do with the cleansing ritual of Islam. For ordinary people, quite obviously only the shoes can be sensibly removed in order to show respect; it would clearly be quite inappropriate to remove your shirt or blouse, trousers or skirt, so the shoes are (as when entering another house) the obvious means of indicating respect.

As mentioned earlier, women are not allowed in the monks' living quarters; nor may they hand anything directly to a monk. If an occasion arises, at a religious ceremony for example, where a woman has to present something to a monk, the monk will spread a piece of cloth in front of him and the object should be placed on this. Women may, however, speak directly to monks who, in Bangkok at least, are only too keen to practise their English. Women should never touch a monk or his robes.

'Visitors to temples should remove their shoes. . .'

8

The Thai Language

ก   ไก่   ก เอ๋ย ก ไก่

ข   ไข่   วางขาย

ค   ควาย ใช้งาน

ฆ   ระฆัง ข้างฝา

ง   งู   เลื้อยคลาน

Introducing the Thai alphabet

The Thais mostly came from China and, not surprisingly, their language is related to Chinese. there are many Thai-speaking peoples (known by the generic description 'Tai') living outside the borders of Thailand, including for example Laos, Vietnam, Yunnan in southern China, Burma and as far afield as Assam in northern India.l

Thai is at root monosyllabic and tonal; that is, the words consist of one syllable and may be spoken in a variety of tones, low, middle or high, rising or falling. With the arrival of Buddhism in Thailand nearly two thousand years ago, Thai acquired a number of polysyllabic words from the Indian languages Sanskrit and Pali which were non-tonal. For

Westerners, these polysyllabic words are easier to pronounce and to remember because they are virtually toneless and because some English words are derived from the same Indo-European root as the Thai word, e.g. *buri*/ borough meaning town. Thai also took a large number of disyllabic words from Khmer, including many words used in the specialized Thai royal language.

ALPHABET

Thai is written from left to right in one continuous stream, without gaps between words and with virtually no punctuation or capital letters. The alphabet is of fairly distant Indian origin and is akin to the Burmese, Lao and Khmer alphabets. There are 44 consonants (but only 28 consonantal sounds), 24 vowels and diphthongs and 4 tone marks (meaning different things for different classes of consonant).

Westerners find it takes a long time to learn to speak or write Thai, and even many of those who have lived most of their lives in Thailand can still only just get by in the spoken language. If it is any consolation, Thais find their own language not that easy to master.

The written language is mainly a question of intellectual effort. The alphabet needs to be learnt and it is so much more complicated than any Western alphabet. Take a few words we have met already:

farang   is written in Thai 'fr^ang'
sanuk   "   "   "   " 'snk'
bpai   "   "   "   " 'aibp it^ao'

Vowels, in short, may be written before, after, above or below the consonant in the same syllable, or in certain combinations of two or three of these positions. This graphic peculiarity takes a long time to absorb. A year's hard study should give you the elements of the alphabet.

SPOKEN LANGUAGE

The spoken language is mainly a problem for Westerners because of the tones. A simple word may mean several things depending on how it is pronounced:

sua (rising) [pronounced like 'sewer'] means a tiger
sua (falling) means a shirt
sua (low tone) means a mat

Here are some of the meanings of the sound '*chai*', with various spellings and tones:

fringe	to pass near	to send
end	to use	to pierce
to blow lightly	man	to spend
to glance	to be	to need
to blend	yes	victory

The tone is as important as the spelling of the word. Both must be learnt together. Westerners tend to make the mistake of learning the word first and hoping they will remember the tone later. Thai children learn both word and tone simultaneously. Better to do it their way.

All consonants at the end of syllables are simplified. When spoken, however they may be spelt, they end only in the hard sounds p, t and k or m, n, ng, w and y. this is why words ending with an l are pronounced final n. 'Oriental Hotel' becomes naturally 'Orienten Hoten' and 'Central Department Store' becomes 'Centren'. The word for 'bill', now used in Thai is 'bin.' In the spoken language, the *l* and *r* in the non-final position are not interchangeable. It is a sign of an educated person if he can get these consonants correct. The most difficult sound for a foreigner is the initial *ng* as there is no equivalent in Western languages.

FORMS OF ADDRESS

Depending on your perceived status and social standing, there are a whole range of personal pronouns in everyday use where in English we use only 'I', 'me' and 'you'. Safe words are *pom* (men only) and *dichan* (women only) for I/me and *khun* for you (men and women). In English, whether you say 'Sir' or 'Ma'am' depends on the sex of the person to whom you are talking. In Thai, it depends on the speaker. A man will always say '*kraap*' and a woman '*kah*' irrespective of the sex of the person spoken to. These two words are used a great deal in Thai since they denote good manners and politeness.

Remember to call men and women by their first (given) name. Almost all Thais have a nickname given to them at birth, usually denoting some characteristic such as 'Black' or 'Fat'. Sometimes it is a tradition. I know a family whose nicknames were 'Tiger, Bear, Elephant, Crocodile and Rhinoceros'. These nicknames stay with you all your life and people are very attached to them. Originally, the only names Thais had were first names; family names were introduced comparatively recently earlier this century, many by Royal Decree of King Vajiravudh (Rama VI). First names are generally very much shorter than family names which may have complex Pali or Sanskrit spellings, but are modernized in pronunciation. The polite form of address is *Khun* for both men and women. Thus you would address Mr Suthep Chantavimol as 'Khun Suthep' and his wife Mrs Pranom Chantavimol as 'Khun Pranom'. So you can see Thailand has had Women's Lib a long time before the West. Khun is used for both men and women, married and unmarried!

Thais, knowing that foreigners find their language almost impossible to learn, will be delighted if you make the effort to say a few words in their language. Here are a few useful phrases:

[r=rising, f=falling, l=low, h=high, no sign=even tone]

VOCABULARY

khop khun maak[f]	thank you very much
kaw[r] toht[f]	sorry, excuse me
mai[f] dee	bad, not good
dee maak[f]	very good
yai kern bpai	too big
lek kem bkai	too small
bpai cha cha	go slowly
bpai rew rew	go quickly
trong bpai	go straight on
liew sai[f]	turn left
liew kwaar[r]	turn right
yood tee[f] thai mai[f] dai[f]	I cannot speak Thai
. . .yoo[l] nai[r]?	Where is. . .?
mai[f] roo	I don't know (a thing)
mai[f] ow	I don't want
prung nee[h]	tomorrow
wan nee[h]	today
mua[f] waan nee[h]	yesterday

nung[l]	one
sawng[r]	two
saam[r]	three
see	four
haa[f]	five
hok[l]	six
tjet[l]	seven
bpaet[l]	eight
gkao[f]	nine
sip[l]	ten
sip[l] *et*	eleven
sip[l] *sawng*[r] etc.	twelve
yii sip[l]	twenty
saam[r] *sip*[l] etc.	thirty
nung[l] *roi*[h]	100
nung[l] *pan*	1,000

9

Did You Know

Thailand has a land area of about 514,000 square kilometres, about the size of France or Texas, and has borders with Burma, Laos, Cambodia and Malaysia. It has direct access to two oceans, the Indian Ocean in the west and the Pacific Ocean in the east.

There are nearly 30,000 Buddhist temples in Thailand, with over 400 located in Bangkok alone. All these temples are in daily use.

In Thai boxing, or *Muay Thai*, the use of fists, elbows, knees, shins and feet is permitted. There are usually five three-minute rounds with two-minute breaks between.

Most Thai males usually enter the monkhood for a period of three months when they reach the age of 25

The name 'Bangkok' means 'Village of the Olives'. The full name of the city is *Krungthep Mahanakorn Bovorn Rattanakosin Mahainthara Ayutthaya Mahadilokob Noparathathani Burirom Udomrajanivej Mahasathani Ampornpiman Avaransathit Sakkatattiya Avisnukamprasit*. Fortunately, this has been shortened to '*Krungthep*' for daily use.